MATT CHRISTOPHER

At the Plate with ...

Mark McGwire

MATT CHRISTOPHER

At the Plate with ...

Mark McGwire

Little, Brown and Company

Boston   New York   London

To Evan Andrew

First Edition

Cover photograph by John Iacono, *Sports Illustrated*/©Time Inc.

Library of Congress Cataloging-in-Publication Data

Christopher, Matt.
    At the plate with . . . Mark McGwire / Matt Christopher. — 1st ed.
       p.   cm.
    Summary: Depicts the life and career of the St. Louis Cardinals slugger, who holds the record for most homeruns in one season.
    ISBN 0-316-13457-0
    1. McGwire, Mark, 1963–   — Juvenile literature.   2. Baseball players — United States — Biography — Juvenile literature.
[1. McGwire, Mark, 1963–   . 2. Baseball players.]   I. Title.
II. Title: Mark McGwire.
GV865.M3123C57   1999
796.357'092 — dc21
[B]   99-13728

10 9 8 7 6 5 4 3 2 1

COM-MO

Printed in the United States of America

Contents

MATT CHRISTOPHER

At the Plate with ...

Mark McGwire

Chapter One:
1963–1981

Learning the Game

During the final months of the 1998 baseball season, Mark McGwire pursued the major league record for most home runs in a season. The same scene took place again and again. Each time he approached the plate, fans stood and cheered.

As Mark dug in to await the pitch, slowly swinging his bat and pointing it toward the pitcher, the cheering grew louder. When the pitcher released the ball, flashbulbs from hundreds of cameras went off all at once as everyone tried to capture one of McGwire's distinctive home-run swings.

Yet despite such distractions, Mark McGwire appeared to be the calmest person in the ballpark. While everyone else wondered whether he would set a new record, McGwire remained focused on the task at hand. All he wanted to do was hit the ball hard.

Nothing else mattered. That may have been what allowed him to achieve what many thought to be impossible.

Hitting a baseball is considered one of the most difficult things to do in sports. To connect with a rapidly spinning ball traveling nearly one hundred miles per hour requires amazing coordination and concentration. Of all the people who have ever tried to hit a baseball, only a few thousand have learned to do so well enough to play in the major leagues.

Hitting a home run is even more difficult. Most major leaguers hit only a few home runs each season. Some come to the plate hundreds of times between home runs.

In order to hit a home run, a batter must do more than just hit the ball — he must hit it perfectly. He must swing the bat fast and at a precise angle, so that the ball makes contact at a very specific place on the bat barrel. If the batter swings a quarter of an inch too low or high, the ball may either pop weakly into the air or dribble slowly along the ground. If he swings too late or too early, the ball goes foul.

A great home-run hitter makes this difficult act appear effortless. When the bat strikes the ball perfectly, a distinctive *crack!* echoes through the ballpark and announces that the hitter has done everything right. The ball takes off as if shot from a gun. Fans can't help but cheer.

George Herman "Babe" Ruth, of the New York Yankees, was baseball's first great home-run hitter. When he retired, in 1935, he held the records for most home runs in a single season, with 60 in 1927, and in a career, with 714.

Ruth's single-season record remained intact until 1961, when the Yankees' Roger Maris hit 61 home runs. In 1974 Hank Aaron became the most prolific home-run hitter of all time when he broke Ruth's career mark, eventually smacking a total of 755 home runs before he retired.

Maris's single-season home-run record became one of baseball's most treasured marks. As the 1998 season began, no one had come close to breaking it. Some people thought the record would never be broken.

Then came Mark McGwire. During the 1998 season he accomplished the impossible. He didn't just break Maris's record, he shattered it, blasting a remarkable 70 home runs and giving baseball fans a season to remember. No one else has ever made hitting a home run seem as effortless as Mark McGwire does.

But even for Mark McGwire, hitting home runs really isn't easy. As he chased the record, McGwire asked reporters over and over, "Do you know how hard it is to hit a home run? Do you have any idea?" They didn't, because Mark McGwire made it look so effortless.

In fact, playing the game of baseball didn't come easy for Mark McGwire. He quit playing once and nearly quit again on several other occasions. He began his career as a pitcher and got a late start as a hitter. He had to overcome several career-threatening injuries and a massive slump that led him to question his own ability.

Yet Mark McGwire was able to persevere because he discovered there was more to life than playing baseball and hitting home runs. He also realized that in order to get the most out of his ability and reach his full potential as a baseball player, he had to learn to believe in himself.

John and Ginger McGwire welcomed their son Mark into the world on October 1, 1963, in Pomona, California. Ironically, on that very day two years earlier, Roger Maris had smacked his record-setting 61st home run.

When Mark's father, John, was growing up, he dreamed of playing in the major leagues or being some other kind of athlete. John's stepfather was a professional boxer. But then one day in 1944, when John was only seven years old, he walked into his house and suddenly collapsed.

His stepfather picked him up and rushed him to the hospital. Doctors discovered that he had polio, a dangerous and contagious viral disease that attacks the nerves. Although the disease is rare today, it was very common before a vaccine was created, in 1954.

Young John was quarantined in a hospital with other polio patients. His family wasn't allowed to visit him for six months. Yet every day they went to the hospital and stood outside so John could wave to them through the window of his room.

When he was finally allowed to go home, the once-healthy boy was crippled. The disease left one leg withered and noticeably shorter than the other. He could walk, but he limped badly.

But John McGwire didn't feel sorry for himself. He grew big and exercised his leg to make it strong. Although he couldn't run well, he discovered that he could still be an athlete. In college, he became a boxer. Later, he took up bicycling and cycled on trips of several hundred miles. He also golfed and played softball. He learned that he could accomplish almost anything if he tried hard enough.

John eventually became a dentist and married a young woman named Ginger, who had been a champion swimmer in high school. The young couple settled in a small house in Pomona, California, and started a family.

They had five sons. They were all strong and athletic, just like their parents. Playing sports was an important part of growing up in the McGwire family. Mark's brother Dan became a quarterback in professional football.

The five boys competed at everything. The family lived at the end of a quiet cul-de-sac, so the boys often used the street as an impromptu athletic field, playing basketball, tennis, and even football on the asphalt.

Golf was the first organized sport Mark played. His father showed him how to hold the clubs and took Mark and his brothers to the local driving range and neighboring courses. Mark loved hitting the ball and watching it soar high and far away.

When he was eight years old, Mark started playing baseball in a developmental league. The league was designed to teach young children the fundamentals of the game, like throwing, catching, and swinging the bat. Winning and losing weren't very important.

Mark liked playing baseball. He was bigger than most of the other kids. He discovered that he could throw the ball fast and hit the ball far, which were the most fun of all.

Two years later, when Mark was ten, he began playing Little League baseball. The first time Mark came to bat in Little League, he saw a pitch he liked, closed his eyes, and swung as hard as he could.

Crack! The bat hitting the ball made a satisfying sound. Mark quickly opened his eyes, surprised that he'd made contact.

He looked for the ball, but all he saw was the out-fielder for the other team standing with his back to the field. The ball had sailed over the fence. With his first swing in Little League, Mark had hit a home run! As Mark's mom remembered later, "I guess that set the tone for him."

Yet Mark soon learned that baseball wasn't always so easy. Because he threw harder than most other kids, Mark played shortstop and pitched. But he didn't always know where the ball was going.

One day while pitching in Little League, Mark just couldn't throw a strike. No matter how hard he tried, he just kept throwing balls. Hitter after hitter walked to first base.

Mark became so frustrated that he began to cry. His father, who was coaching the team, finally felt sorry for him and had Mark switch positions with the shortstop. As Mark tried to sniff away his tears, he noticed that home plate looked fuzzy. After the game, he told his father he was having trouble seeing.

Mark's dad took him to an eye doctor. He examined Mark's eyes and discovered that he needed glasses. Mark noticed an immediate improvement in his play when he wore the glasses.

Today, Mark still needs glasses, although he usually wears contact lenses during games. When you see Mark standing in the batter's box, looking at the pitcher and blinking, he's trying to clear his contact lenses.

As Mark grew older, people started telling his parents that he might have a chance to play professional baseball. Although that made Mr. and Mrs. McGwire feel proud of their son, they never made a big deal out of it. They didn't want Mark to feel as if he had to play baseball. They just wanted him to have fun.

Although Mark liked playing baseball, it wasn't his favorite sport. He loved playing golf even more. He hardly paid attention to major league baseball, but he followed professional golf closely.

When Mark reached high school at Damien High in Claremont, California, he was already more than six feet tall and weighed two hundred pounds. Everyone expected him to be a star on the baseball team.

But Damien was a large school, and it was difficult for young players to make the team. As a sophomore, Mark was still on the junior varsity team. He wasn't playing much and wasn't very excited about baseball.

Then Mark pulled a chest muscle. He also got sick with mononucleosis, a common viral disease that causes weariness, among other symptoms. While he recuperated, he wasn't allowed to take batting practice. Since baseball season would be almost over by the time he recovered, Mark decided to quit the baseball team and join the golf team instead.

He was an immediate success and won several tournaments. But Mark was surprised to discover that he missed playing baseball. That summer he put down his golf clubs and picked up the bat again.

In 1980, in his junior year at Damien, he made the varsity baseball team. Mark threw nearly ninety miles per hour and had good control for a high school pitcher. He became an important member of Coach John Carrol's team.

Pro scouts attended Damien's games and told Coach Carrol that Mark had the potential to pitch in professional baseball. Carrol knew Mark's chances might be ruined if he got hurt during a game. So when Mark wasn't pitching, the world's greatest home-run hitter sat on the bench! "That's how brilliant we were as coaches," says Carrol today, laughing.

Mark pitched well his junior year, and in his limited opportunities at the plate, he made an impression. Coach Carrol often tells the story about a home run Mark hit at the Ganesha High School field in Pomona: "The fence there is approximately three hundred fifteen to three hundred twenty feet down the line, then it's forty feet high. I saw Mark put one over that and onto a house the fence is supposed to protect. It hit the house and kept going down the street. It's the longest home run I've ever seen hit."

Mark was beginning to take baseball more seriously. He helped lead his American Legion team to the state finals, and he even threw a no-hitter during the tournament. At home with his brothers, Mark spent every moment working on his game, hitting a Wiffle ball off a tee to perfect his swing or throwing a baseball to improve his accuracy.

In Mark's senior year, he asked Coach Carrol if he

could play when he wasn't pitching. He didn't like sitting on the bench. Carrol agreed. There was no way he could keep a batter with Mark's power on the bench. Now, when he wasn't pitching, Mark got to play first base.

Mark thrived during his senior season. He fielded well at first base, and at the plate he hit a team-best .359 with five home runs. On the mound he was even better. His record was 5 and 3 and his ERA was a stellar 1.90.

College coaches and professional scouts were impressed. They didn't think much of Mark as a hitter, despite his five home runs, but his ninety-mile-per-hour fastball got their attention. Both Arizona State University and the University of Southern California (USC) wanted Mark on their pitching staff. Both offered him a baseball scholarship.

Mark hadn't really considered college before the scholarship offer. He was merely an average student in high school and didn't pay much attention in class. "I just liked to sit in the back and blend in," he once told a sportswriter. But now he began to think about his future.

At about the same time, Mark was drafted by the

Montreal Expos in the eighth round of baseball's 1981 free-agent draft. The Expos wanted Mark to sign a professional contract and start playing minor league baseball as soon as he finished high school.

At first Mark didn't know what to do. He was intrigued by the possibility of playing pro ball. But the Expos didn't want to give Mark very much money to turn professional. They told scout Jack Paepke to offer only a $5,000 bonus.

Paepke knew the offer wasn't very good and that Mark was not likely to accept it. When he met with Mark and his parents, he said to Mark, "I think you should go to school." Mark and his parents agreed. The Expos' offer simply didn't compare with the value of a college education.

Mark turned the Expos down and accepted the scholarship from the University of Southern California. The school was close to home, so his parents could watch him play. If he continued to improve and pitched well for USC, Mark was certain he would receive another opportunity to play professional baseball. Playing baseball, he thought at the time, was easy.

Chapter Two:
1981–1984

From Pitcher's Mound to Batter's Box

Attending college changed Mark's life. He discovered that he had to take his studies seriously and pay attention in order to succeed. If he didn't keep his grades up, he would not be eligible to play baseball.

Mark was surprised to discover that he actually enjoyed school and liked learning about new things. He decided to major in public administration and even thought about entering politics one day. In the meantime, he enjoyed living in a dormitory and meeting people from all over the country.

But most of all, Mark liked playing baseball. Under legendary coach Rod Dedeaux, the University of Southern California had one of the best collegiate baseball programs in the country. The Trojans had won the College World Series several times, and dozens of Dedeaux's players had gone on to careers in professional baseball. Some, like pitcher Tom Seaver and outfielder Fred Lynn, had become stars.

Trojans pitching coach Marcel Lachemann took McGwire under his wing and tried to turn him into a solid college pitcher. In high school, Mark was able to get by primarily on his fastball. Few high school hitters could catch up to the pitch.

But in college, every player was a former high school star. Mark couldn't get by on just a fastball. He had to learn to throw the ball to spots and develop other pitches, such as a curveball and slider.

The Trojans decided to bring Mark along slowly. In his freshman year he was primarily a relief pitcher, throwing only two or three innings at a time.

Mark did much better than expected. Many freshman pitchers struggle with control and give up a lot of runs. But in twenty appearances in forty-seven innings, Mark more than held his own, winning four games and losing four, with an ERA of only 3.04, a good figure for a college pitcher. He struck out 31 and walked 29.

The Trojans were impressed. So were major league scouts. Mark had grown to six feet five inches tall. Scouts liked big pitchers who could throw hard.

Mark's bat began to attract notice as well. He had subbed in a few times at first base and as designated hitter for the Trojans and hit .200 in 75 at bats, with three home runs. He wasn't a great hitter, but compared with most pitchers, he was more than adequate.

Those stats were strong enough to impress Trojans hitting coach Ron Vaughn. In batting practice Mark showed tremendous power. Vaughn wondered how well Mark might be able to hit if he turned all his attention toward hitting.

After the end of the season, in June 1982, Vaughn received a call from Jim Dietz, the baseball coach at San Diego State University. He asked Vaughn to serve as his assistant that summer in the Alaskan Summer League, a league for college players.

Vaughn readily agreed. The two men then began to discuss the roster of their team, the Glacier Pilots.

Dietz still needed a few more players. "What else are you looking for?" asked Vaughn.

"A power-hitting first baseman," replied Dietz.

Vaughn had an idea. "I know one," he said. "Mark McGwire."

Dietz was puzzled. He knew the name but thought

of McGwire as a pitcher. "Are you sure?" he asked Vaughn.

"I think he can be an outstanding hitter," replied Vaughn. That was good enough for Dietz. A few days later Vaughn asked Mark if he wanted to play in Alaska. Mark agreed. Although he wouldn't get to pitch, he'd still be playing baseball.

But soon after Mark arrived in Anchorage, Alaska, home of the Pilots, he got depressed and homesick. Anchorage was nothing like Southern California. Even in the summer, the temperature barely topped seventy degrees and it was often damp. The Pilots' home field wasn't very well maintained. In addition, Mark was trying to play a new position. In his first few games he struggled at the plate. Pitching had always come naturally to Mark. Hitting was much harder.

McGwire wanted to quit and go home. "I was away from home for the first time in my life," Mark remembered later. "I went through a very bad period of homesickness." But Dietz spoke with Mark's father, and John McGwire thought Mark should stick it out. Mark reluctantly agreed.

Vaughn worked with him in the batting cage for

17

hours every day, teaching him how to become a hitter. In particular, Vaughn worked on Mark's swing, trying to make it shorter and more compact. Because Mark was big, he tended to swing big and take a big looping cut at the ball. When he made contact, he hit the ball hard. But he was easily fooled and sometimes missed badly. Vaughn knew that Mark was strong enough that he could cut down his swing, hit for a higher average, and still hit home runs.

Vaughn was right. Mark soon started hitting the ball.

He finished the summer season with a .403 average with 13 home runs and 53 RBIs. That was more than good. It was great!

When Mark returned to USC in the fall, he told coach Dedeaux that he didn't really want to pitch anymore. "I'm a pretty good player when I can concentrate on one thing only," he said.

Dedeaux wasn't completely convinced. Besides, the Trojans needed pitchers. Dedeaux had recruited a new pitcher, a six-foot-ten-inch phenom named Randy Johnson, but Johnson was still raw and needed time to develop. Mark McGwire had experience.

When practice began, Dedeaux soon saw that Mark had improved greatly at the plate. Although he still wanted Mark to pitch, he also agreed to let him hit and play first base.

Mark thrived under the workload. On the mound, he was one of the team's best pitchers. In eight starts he went 3 and 1 and lowered his ERA to 2.78. But at the plate, he was a monster!

Mark crushed the ball. He slammed 19 home runs to set a new school record, breaking the mark once held by major leaguer and USC alum Dave Hostetler. He still struck out too often and didn't hit for a very high average, but his power potential was unmistakable. By the end of his sophomore season, Mark was a full-time hitter. Pitching was in his past.

Now Mark could turn his full attention to hitting. He worked out all summer long and when he reported for practice his junior year, he had improved even more.

During his sophomore season, Mark's batting prowess had surprised the opposition. Now, a year later, they thought they were ready for him.

Pitchers had become so wary of Mark's power that they had started throwing him very few fastballs.

Like most power hitters, Mark loved fastballs and had gotten most of his hits the previous year off them. This year, the pitchers tried to trick him by throwing mostly curveballs and change-ups.

Mark adjusted easily. Under Vaughn's tutelage, he had learned to wait on the ball. It didn't matter to Mark what the pitchers threw him. He hit everything!

He led college baseball with 32 home runs and hit .387 with 80 RBIs. Moreover, he struck out only 33 times.

Mark wasn't a homesick, struggling player anymore. He was one of the best amateur players in the country and everyone knew it. The *Sporting News* named him the collegiate Player of the Year.

In 1984, baseball was scheduled to be a demonstration sport at the Olympics before becoming a full-fledged event in 1988. It was the first time since 1964 that baseball would be featured at the Games. Rod Dedeaux was named coach of the Olympic team.

He picked the best players in college baseball for the American team. To no one's surprise, Mark McGwire was one of his selections. The team also included such future major league stars as shortstop Barry Larkin, who later played for the Cincinnati Reds, and first baseman Will Clark, who later starred for the San Francisco Giants and Texas Rangers. McGwire and Clark shared the first-base job on the team.

The 1984 U.S. Olympic baseball team was one of the greatest amateur teams ever put together. Of the twenty players Dedeaux selected, seventeen eventually played major league baseball.

But playing Olympic ball wasn't the only thing on Mark's mind that summer. College baseball players become eligible for the major league draft after their junior season. Mark McGwire was one of the most sought-after players in the draft. As he toured with the Olympians, he waited to learn his fate in professional baseball.

The Oakland Athletics were only one of many teams interested in Mark. The New York Mets, with the first pick in the draft, also wanted him. Most scouts concurred with the appraisal of A's scouting director Dick Wiencek, who described Mark as the "best power hitter in the country. Should be the number one pick."

But the A's picked tenth and didn't think they had a chance of getting McGwire. They were certain he would be gone by the time it was their turn to choose.

The Mets planned to draft Mark first and contacted him before the draft. But McGwire wouldn't commit to signing a contract. He wasn't sure if he wanted to play for a team on the East Coast, so far from home.

On draft day, the A's were surprised when the Mets used their pick to select Shawn Abner, a high school outfielder. Then, incredibly, the next eight teams also passed over Mark to select other players.

The A's jumped at their chance and selected Mark with their first pick, number ten overall.

McGwire was thrilled to be selected by a team in California. But before he could talk with the A's, he had a few other things to do. First, he married his girlfriend, Kathy. The two had met at USC when Kathy worked as a ball girl retrieving foul balls at the ballpark. Then, he had to play in the Olympics, held that year in Los Angeles. Team USA was an overwhelming favorite to win the gold medal.

As the team toured the country playing a series of

exhibitions to prepare for the Olympics, McGwire wowed observers by putting on a one-man power show. In a game at Fenway Park, he hit a long drive to center field that nearly went out of the ballpark. Star slugger Reggie Jackson was on the bench that day and told Dedeaux: "That's the longest ball I've ever seen hit." When Dedeaux mentioned that McGwire was using an aluminum bat, standard in collegiate and international play, Jackson just shook his head. "I don't care what kind of bat it is," he said. "I've never seen anything that far."

When the Olympics began, Team USA rolled through the round-robin portion of the eight-team tournament, compiling a 3 and 0 record to qualify for the medal round. Then they defeated Korea 5–2 to qualify for the gold-medal game against Japan.

In the months before the Games, the U.S. team had played seven exhibitions against Japan and compiled a 6–1 record. Everyone thought the United States would win easily.

But the Japanese were the more experienced team. They had played together for a much longer time. They weren't intimidated by the U.S. squad.

Japan's pitchers shut down Mark and his teammates

on only seven hits, and when a Japanese player hit a three-run home run in the eighth inning, they took command of the game. Japan won, 6–3. McGwire and Team USA had to settle for a silver medal.

McGwire was disappointed, but he had little time to feel sorry. As soon as the Olympics were over, he signed with the Oakland A's for a $150,000 bonus to play professional baseball.

It was time to get even more serious about baseball.

Chapter Three:
1984–1986

Minor Problems

Minor league baseball is divided into divisions rang-
ing from rookie leagues for the most inexperienced
players to triple-A for those players who are nearly
ready for the major leagues. Although the 1984 season was nearly over by the time Mark signed his
contract that summer, the Athletics sent him to their
single-A minor league team in Modesto, California,
at the beginning of August.

Still, playing professional baseball at any level is
much different from playing collegiate baseball.
Teams play almost every day and travel for hours by
bus from one city to another. Many players live on
their own for the first time.

McGwire's Olympic experience had helped to
prepare him for the rigors of minor league life,
but he still had to make adjustments. The most

important change for McGwire was learning to swing a wooden bat.

In most youth, scholastic, and collegiate baseball programs, players use aluminum bats. They don't break, and a single bat often lasts an entire season.

But aluminum bats are also more lively and forgiving than wooden bats. A ball hit by an aluminum bat travels faster and farther than one hit with wood, and precisely where the ball strikes the bat is less significant. A ball hit on the trademark of a wooden bat, for instance, is usually a weak ground ball or a pop-up. To go far, the ball must be hit on the "sweet spot," a small area on the barrel of the bat. With an aluminum bat, a trademark hit can still be a base hit.

As a result, many amateur players get into bad habits at the plate. It is sometimes difficult for scouts to project how well players will hit when they make the transition to wooden bats. Some players, even those picked in the first round, are unable to adjust.

When Mark arrived at Modesto, manager George Mitterwald later recalled, "He wasn't as aggressive [at the plate] as he was in college. There's always a period of getting used to a wooden bat." Mark also was recovering from a pulled hamstring muscle that affected his swing.

He appeared in sixteen games in Modesto before the season ended, coming to bat only 55 times and collecting 11 hits. He hit only one home run.

McGwire was shocked by his poor performance and began to doubt his own ability. He told his wife, "I can't hit anymore. I've lost it. I've got to quit."

Fortunately, Kathy McGwire was able to persuade her husband to keep trying. But he was still insecure over his ability.

The Athletics' minor league system was loaded with talented young players, such as Jose Canseco, McGwire's teammate at Modesto. McGwire knew he would have to work extra hard to keep up. In the off-season, he spent hours trying to adjust to the wooden bat, swinging at a ball on a tee and in a batting cage.

When Mark arrived for spring training in 1985, he was much more prepared than he had been the previous summer. But his confidence quickly vanished when he found out what the Athletics had in mind.

In addition to McGwire, the A's had another power-hitting first-base prospect, Rob Nelson. They wanted both young men to play as much as possible and hoped that one day both would play for the A's in the major leagues.

Since McGwire had a strong arm and had played shortstop when he was younger, the A's switched his position to third base. The move left McGwire puzzled.

Instead of viewing the switch as positive, he wondered if the A's had lost faith in him. Still, he worked hard to make the transition. Third base is a more demanding position to play than first base. Mark took hundreds of ground balls every day, trying to get comfortable with the change.

At the end of spring training, the A's returned McGwire to Modesto. Although he felt more comfortable at the plate, he still worried about his fielding. The Athletics wanted him to throw straight over the top, whereas McGwire was more comfortable throwing from a three-quarters angle. He struggled to make the change.

Despite the adjustments he had to make to his throw, he had a breakout year at bat. He learned to hit the ball on the sweet spot and his power reemerged. He led the league with 24 home runs and 106 RBIs. Although he made 33 errors at third base, he led the league in total fielding chances accepted, which meant he was getting to every ball he should get to, even if he wasn't always successful in throwing the batter out.

His performance put him on a fast track to the major leagues. The A's realized that McGwire was one of their top prospects, a rare player who hit for both power and a good batting average.

In 1986 he was promoted to their double-A team, in Huntsville, Alabama, in the Southern League. Many players have a difficult time making the transition from single-A to double-A. Almost every player is considered a top prospect and the competition is much stiffer. As a hitter, McGwire would be facing better pitching than he had at Modesto.

He soon discovered he had little trouble hitting the ball. Pitchers in double-A were no more successful in getting him out than those in single-A.

Unlike most power hitters, McGwire didn't always pull the ball. Instead, he hit it where it was pitched: pulling the inside pitch, taking the ball over the plate up the middle, and driving the outside pitch to right field. Moreover, his strength and quick bat allowed him to hit with power to all fields. Pitchers still tried to get him out with curves, sliders, and change-ups, but McGwire was patient at the plate and not easily fooled. He didn't strike out as much as most young sluggers.

But although he was enjoying a fine season at the plate, he was less than comfortable at third base. "I don't know if his heart was really in it," recalled Huntsville manager Mark Fischer. "Mac found it real frustrating to play third base." Too many of McGwire's throws skipped past the first baseman or sailed over his head. Despite his fine performance at the plate, McGwire was plagued by self-doubt. He worried that his defensive problems would keep him out of the big leagues.

The A's had no such worries. After only two months of the season, McGwire was tearing up the league, hitting over .300 with 10 home runs and more than 50 RBIs. The previous year, the A's had promoted Jose Canseco in midseason from Huntsville to their triple-A team, in Tacoma, Washington, after he had similar success. Canseco had gone on to hit just as well in triple-A and was now one of the top rookies in the major leagues.

The A's decided to do the same with McGwire. He was promoted to Tacoma, only one step away from the major leagues.

He battered Pacific Coast League pitching. In seventy-eight games, he hit .318 and smacked 13 home runs.

But he still struggled in the field. The harder he tried, the worse he played. In those seventy-eight games, he was charged with 25 errors, mostly on throws, which is an average of approximately one error every three games. Although his bat was major league quality, his play at third was substandard.

Still, the A's thought enough of their young slugger that on August 20, 1986, McGwire received the news that all young professional ballplayers dream of hearing. Tacoma manager Keith Lieppman called him into his office and told McGwire the Athletics wanted him to join them in Baltimore. It would be Mark's first major league game.

McGwire rushed to the airport and flew to Baltimore but was disappointed when the game was rained out. The A's then traveled to New York. As he warmed up for their first game, on August 22, McGwire glanced at the lineup card that A's manager Tony LaRussa had posted in the clubhouse.

McGwire couldn't believe his eyes. He was starting at third base!

Like many rookies, McGwire was in a daze in his first game. He was nervous and overanxious at the plate, and he went hitless. But LaRussa was determined to get a good look at the prospect. He kept McGwire in the lineup, even after he went hitless in his second start.

In the final game of the series, the A's faced veteran Yankees pitcher Tommy John. Although John didn't throw hard, he was a great pitcher. He had fabulous control, using a combination of sinking fastballs, curves, sliders, and sinkers to get the opposition to hit into easy ground outs. John usually had little trouble with big sluggers, particularly young players who lacked the discipline to lay off his pitches out of the strike zone.

But McGwire wasn't like most young hitters. He wasn't as nervous as he had been in his first two games, and he showed great patience at the plate, taking what John would give him and not trying to pull pitches on the outside corner. As the A's romped to an 11–4 win, McGwire collected three hits. He didn't care that they weren't home runs. He was just glad to have his first major league hits under his belt.

From New York, the A's traveled to Detroit to play the Tigers. McGwire was feeling more comfortable.

On the evening of August 25, McGwire took to the field again, playing third and batting eighth in the order. On the mound for Detroit was Walt Terrell. Like John, Terrell was a finesse pitcher. In his last start, he almost pitched a no-hitter.

Terrell wasn't as sharp this day. Entering the fifth inning, he had already given up three runs. The game was tied.

McGwire had gone hitless in his first two at bats. Terrell had thrown him sliders low and away. When McGwire came up in the fifth with a man on base, the pitcher decided to challenge the rookie.

He threw a fastball up and over the plate. McGwire swung.

Crack! He connected with the pitch on the sweet spot of the bat.

The ball took off toward center field. Tigers

center fielder Chet Lemon turned and raced toward the fence. At 440 feet from home plate, it was the most distant fence in the major leagues.

Lemon turned and looked for the ball. He slowed to a trot, then stopped and watched.

The high fly just kept going. The ball sailed over Lemon's head and over the fence, clattering into the stands well beyond the fence. Only a handful of players had ever hit the ball over the center-field fence at Tiger Stadium before.

McGwire, who had been running hard, saw the umpire give the home-run signal and slowed as he reached first base.

McGwire had just hit his first major league home run!

The A's went on to win, 8–4. After the game, the press crowded around McGwire's locker, asking him about his home run. "I don't know if I've hit one farther," he said with a smile. "I really can't say. They had been working me away with sliders, but this pitch was up."

The hit gave McGwire confidence. He knew he could hit major league pitching.

But McGwire continued to struggle at third base. Although he hit two more home runs by the end of the season, he fielded poorly, making six errors.

There was still room for improvement.

Chapter Four:
1987

Rookie Record

When McGwire arrived at spring training in March 1987, he was determined to prove that he belonged in the major leagues. The A's were rebuilding, and manager Tony LaRussa wanted to give young players a chance to prove themselves. The previous season, Jose Canseco had smacked 33 home runs and won the Rookie of the Year award.

That was a good situation for McGwire, but at the same time, the Oakland club had many talented young players. The A's were still convinced that McGwire's future was at third base, but he worried that his defensive shortcomings would prevent him from making the team.

With veteran slugger Reggie Jackson leading the way, the A's worked hard in spring training. No rookie worked harder than Mark McGwire.

LaRussa was impressed and later said he'd never seen a young hitter "so fundamentally sound." When McGwire got off to a quick start in the exhibition season, LaRussa paid attention. McGwire found himself in the lineup nearly every day. He occasionally played third, but when he continued to have trouble throwing the ball, LaRussa gave him more and more time at first base and as designated hitter. Besides, A's veteran Carney Lansford was one of the best third basemen in baseball.

McGwire's hot bat forced him into the lineup. He ended the exhibition season with a batting average of over .300 and 32 RBIs. At the end of spring training LaRussa announced that he planned to platoon McGwire at first base with fellow rookie Rob Nelson. That meant the left-handed-swinging Nelson would bat against right-handed pitching, while the reverse would be true for the right-handed-swinging McGwire.

But in the first few weeks of the season, both Nelson and McGwire slumped. LaRussa came to the conclusion that the platoon was bothering both players. Neither was getting enough playing time to get into a groove.

McGwire had hit slightly better than Nelson and had not struck out as often, so on April 20 LaRussa sent Nelson to the minor leagues and gave the first-base job to McGwire. Mark was happy but knew that if he didn't start hitting, he might soon trade places with Nelson.

The move helped McGwire relax. By being in the lineup every day, he didn't have much time to dwell on any failures. There was always the next game to look forward to.

In May, McGwire caught fire. He crushed 15 home runs for the month, only one short of the major league record held by Mickey Mantle.

All of a sudden, McGwire was one of the biggest stories in baseball. The press surrounded his locker after nearly every game.

They quickly learned that he was just as special off the field as he was at the plate. The quiet young slugger appeared to be a genuinely nice young man. At the end of the interviews, he said "Thank you." Most ballplayers are much more standoffish.

One writer was so impressed that he even wrote a letter to McGwire's parents. He told them they should be proud of their son and congratulated them for raising such a nice young man. A's coach Jim Lefebvre later said, "He had an attitude you'd like to copy and distribute to all young players."

American League pitchers didn't have quite the same reaction. Mark McGwire was making their lives miserable.

By the All-Star break McGwire had belted 33 home runs. The rookie home-run record of 38 was well within reach. Some people even thought McGwire had a chance to break Roger Maris's single-season home-run record of 61. To no one's surprise, McGwire was named to the All-Star team as a reserve, a rare honor for a rookie.

But McGwire didn't let all the attention go to his head. He downplayed talk of setting records. All he would say about his remarkable performance was that it was "pretty neat."

"I don't do anything special," he told a reporter. "Just see the ball, hit the ball, and be aggressive."

That season, the A's were one of the most exciting teams in baseball. In addition to McGwire, fellow rookies Terry Steinbach and Luis Polonia were also playing well. Fans became accustomed to seeing either McGwire, who hit fourth, or teammate Jose

Canseco, batting third, smack long home runs and congratulate each other by bashing their forearms together. The press nicknamed the duo the "Bash Brothers."

McGwire's home-run pace slacked off in July, then slowed to a crawl in August. He admitted that all the extra attention he was receiving disrupted his concentration. Although he hit his 39th long ball of the season and broke the rookie home-run record on August 14, he entered September with only 40 home runs.

He was also distracted by another event. His wife, Kathy, was pregnant. The McGwires' first child was due at the end of September.

Talk of catching Roger Maris faded. So too did all the attention from the press, now that McGwire held the rookie record. With the A's in the race for the division championship, McGwire was able to re-gain his focus. He went on another home-run tear, smacking 9 more home runs to bring his total to 49.

Now the press turned its attention back to McGwire. He still had a chance to hit 50 home runs, a single-season mark reached by only ten players in the history of the game.

With only two games remaining in the season, the A's were on the road and McGwire was stuck on 49 home runs. Then he received a call from Kathy. She was going into labor.

McGwire immediately contacted LaRussa and asked for permission to return to California to be with his wife for the birth of their child. Hitting 50 home runs wasn't nearly as important as that.

Though the A's were in a late-season slump, LaRussa readily agreed. McGwire made it to the hospital less than an hour before his son, Matthew, was born. Although he was later named Rookie of the Year, nothing that happened in the 1987 season could compare to the way he felt about being a father.

But he began to realize that his life had changed dramatically. With his distinctive red hair and ruddy complexion, he was easily recognized whenever he went out in public, and the demands of the press seemed unrelenting. A naturally shy person, all the attention made him increasingly uncomfortable.

"I don't want to be just the baseball player," he told a reporter. "I want to be myself." For Mark McGwire, continuing to be himself would prove to be the biggest challenge of all.

Chapter Five:
1988–1991

Ups and Downs

McGwire worked out hard in the off-season. He knew that many rookies experience what is called the "sophomore jinx," or a letdown in their second season. He didn't want that to happen to him. The year had been very good. But he knew that everyone was wondering if he could do it again.

For the first time, McGwire started lifting weights. He wanted to become stronger and not to wear down as the season progressed. He also began paying more attention to his diet and started taking vitamins and dietary supplements.

When he arrived at spring training, his teammates could hardly believe he was the same person. He had added more than fifteen pounds of muscle. He had once looked rangy. But now he was muscular.

Once more, people began to ask him if he could break the home-run record.

He found such talk increasingly tiresome. The young man who had been so polite to the press as a rookie now turned curt and testy. He believed that talk about individual performances was inappropriate. Baseball, he kept reminding everyone, was a team game.

The 1988 A's were a strong team. The addition of veteran pitchers Storm Davis and Bob Welch solidified the pitching staff, and reliever Dennis Eckersley emerged as the best closer in baseball. With the Bash Brothers leading the way, the A's jumped into first place and never looked back.

Yet despite all his work in the off-season, McGwire couldn't match his first-year performance. He finished the season with 32 home runs and 99 RBIs. For any other twenty-four-year-old in baseball, it would have been a great season. But for McGwire, it was viewed as a disappointment.

He felt distracted all year. He and Kathy separated, then got back together, only to separate again. He tried not to allow his personal problems to affect his play, but it was hard. McGwire kept all his worries inside as he tried to focus on the upcoming playoffs.

The Western Division champion A's played the Boston Red Sox for the American League pennant. They swept Boston in four games. McGwire had a good series, hitting .333 with a home run, but was overshadowed by Canseco, who hit three home runs. That was fine with McGwire. All he cared about was that the A's were going to the World Series.

Oakland entered the Series as the heavy favorite over the National League champion Los Angeles Dodgers. But in the first game, with Oakland leading 4–3 in the ninth inning, injured Dodgers slugger Kirk Gibson came off the bench to hit a dramatic two-run, game-ending home run off Eckersley. The Dodgers won game one, 5–4.

Oakland never recovered. Led by pitcher Orel Hershiser, the Dodgers won three of the next four games to win the Series.

Like most Oakland hitters, McGwire had slumped. In 17 at bats, he had only one hit, a home run. He and his wife had split for good just before the Series started. He never used it as an excuse, but the breakup bothered him.

McGwire was disappointed the A's hadn't won the World Series, but he believed the A's were still one of the best teams in baseball and was determined to prove it to the world.

His teammates agreed. In 1989, despite the loss of Jose Canseco for much of the season due to injury, Oakland picked up right where they left off and cruised to another division championship.

McGwire battled back problems all year caused by a herniated disk. He still managed to crack another 33 home runs and knock in almost 100 RBIs, but his batting average slumped to .231.

This time the A's played the Toronto Blue Jays for the American League pennant. They won in five games; Mark hit .389 and smacked a home run.

Their victory set up a Bay Area World Series, as the San Francisco Giants won the National League pennant. McGwire's three hits in game one in Oakland paced the A's to a 5–0 win. Then Oakland won game two 5–1 to take a commanding two-games-to-none lead.

The Series moved to San Francisco for game

three. But as the two clubs warmed up before the game, the unthinkable happened. The Bay Area was rocked by a powerful earthquake that collapsed highways and buildings throughout the region. Fortunately, no one at San Francisco's Candlestick Park was seriously hurt in the quake, but the Series was postponed for ten days while the area recovered and structural damage was repaired at the ballpark.

When the Series resumed, the A's came out swinging, blasting the Giants 13–7 and 9–6 to sweep the Series and become world champions.

But instead of rushing onto the field, climbing all over one another, spraying one another with champagne, and having a victory parade, the A's celebration was subdued. A number of people had died in the earthquake and the team didn't want to be insensitive.

McGwire, who hit .294 in the Series, was thrilled to be a member of a world championship team. But at the same time, he was troubled.

Despite cracking 65 home runs during the past two seasons, he was concerned about his drooping batting average and his nagging back problems. But that wasn't all.

McGwire simply wasn't happy. Even though he was a baseball star and had signed a big contract worth $1.5 million for the upcoming season, he was dissatisfied with his life and the person he had become. Becoming a big star had taken a toll on him and his family.

McGwire wasn't as trusting anymore. He now questioned the motives of people who wanted to hang out with him. Yet at the same time, in some ways, he tried to act like a big star. He was confused and didn't know how to act. Even baseball, the game he loved, wasn't bringing him enjoyment. Still, with nothing else to concentrate on, Mark focused on the game.

In 1990, the A's rolled to yet another division championship, winning 103 games. Canseco came back to hit 37 home runs and knock in 101, and pitcher Bob Welch won 27 games.

When he hit 39 home runs, McGwire set a record by becoming the first player in baseball history to hit 30 or more home runs in each of his first four seasons in the major leagues. But his batting average was only .235. Oakland fans began to boo him.

McGwire was a victim of unrealistic expectations. After his rookie year, everyone expected him to be another Babe Ruth. But he couldn't be Ruth. All he could be was Mark McGwire. But he wasn't even sure who Mark McGwire was anymore. The harder he tried, the more he seemed to flag. Baseball wasn't as fun as it once was.

Even winning another division championship left McGwire with a hollow feeling. As he later explained to a writer, "It bothered me when nobody ran on the field and jumped on top of each other after we won the AL West." The A's, and even McGwire, took their success for granted.

Although the A's again defeated the Red Sox in the League Championship Series to win their third consecutive pennant, the underdog Cincinnati Reds swept the A's in the World Series. McGwire had a terrible postseason, collecting only five hits, all singles. He felt as if he had let everyone down, including himself.

McGwire and the A's downhill slide continued in 1991. The team's pitching never got on track and McGwire slumped all year long.

Every time he looked in the newspaper or glanced

at the scoreboard when he stepped to the plate, he became disgusted with himself. His average hovered around .200, and now, for the first time, his power suffered as well.

He blamed himself for the A's poor record and continued to blame himself for the breakup of his marriage. He worried about the effect it would have on his son, Matthew. And he worried that his career was over. He wondered if his early success had been a fluke. He knew that neither the A's nor any other team in baseball would continue to have any interest in a player who could barely hit .200.

When he went to the plate, he was hounded by self-doubt. Instead of thinking about success, he worried about failure. Instead of trying to hit the ball hard, he worried about striking out. He found it impossible to concentrate, and without total concentration, it's almost impossible to hit major league pitching. He was in a long downward spiral.

Near the end of the season, as he nursed a .201 batting average, McGwire asked Tony LaRussa to remove him from the lineup. He was afraid his average would fall below .200. His self-confidence was shot.

McGwire finished the 1991 season with only 22 home runs. The A's finished fourth.

He felt as if he had reached rock bottom. In the off-season the A's tried to trade him, but no other team in baseball wanted him. They all thought Mark McGwire was washed up.

McGwire didn't blame them. He felt that way, too.

Chapter Six:
1992-1995

Comebacks

After the 1991 season, McGwire drove alone from Oakland back to his home in Los Angeles. During the long, five-hour journey, he assessed his life. He didn't like what he found.

He was terribly unhappy. His thoughts turned to how his father had suffered as a child, how he hadn't had a chance to fulfill his dream of becoming a major league player.

Mark knew he had to make a decision. Did he really want to continue playing baseball, and if so, was he willing to do whatever was needed to resurrect his career? He knew that unless he was totally committed to rebuilding his career, he would fail.

McGwire sensed that his slump had little to do with his swing or some other kind of technical problem. There were times he still hit the ball as well as ever. The major problem, he thought, was in his head. Too often, he went to the plate distracted by a hundred different things, such as his personal problems. He was unable to concentrate, and without concentration, he had no confidence and was unable to hit the ball consistently.

McGwire decided that he needed to find out why he was so unhappy. When he got home, he put his bags down on the floor, walked over to the telephone, and made an appointment with a psychiatrist.

Psychiatrists are medical doctors trained in the study and treatment of mental, emotional, or behavioral problems. Most of their patients are simply troubled by something.

McGwire was indeed troubled. In his therapy sessions with the psychiatrist, he began to understand that he had been hiding his emotions and burying his feelings. When things were going badly for McGwire, he never let on or confided in anyone. Growing up in a family of five boys reinforced the incorrect notion that feelings were a sign of weakness.

McGwire's inability to open up meant that all

his feelings became bottled up inside. He became aware that this was the reason he was so unhappy and why he found it so hard to concentrate. As McGwire later admitted, "I didn't know how to communicate."

Slowly at first, McGwire's therapist won his trust and got him to talk about his problems. McGwire began to open up and realize that it was all right for a major league baseball player to feel sad sometimes and to cry. He didn't have to be Superman. Just being Mark McGwire was good enough.

Those realizations helped McGwire immeasurably. He began to express his feelings more openly.

In only one example, he mended his relationship with his ex-wife. They didn't remarry, but McGwire was able to get beyond his anger and frustration with himself over their breakup and to focus on how he and Kathy had to work together for the benefit of their son. When Kathy remarried, McGwire eventually became friends with her new husband. The two men play golf together regularly and McGwire often joins the family on outings.

Therapy taught McGwire to deal with his problems and prevent them from becoming a distraction.

McGwire eventually spent four years in therapy and still had much to learn about himself, but he made enough progress during the 1991 off-season that he was able to concentrate on baseball again.

He got into the best physical condition of his life. He shared an apartment with his younger brother, Jay, who had been a promising athlete before being shot in the eye with a BB gun. After the accident, he had become a bodybuilder. But Jay began abusing illegal steroids, dangerous drugs that promote muscle growth. Luckily, Jay sought help for his problem before the drugs destroyed him.

As Jay recovered, he and Mark began to work out together. McGwire also began doing special exercises designed to strengthen his vision. When he arrived at spring training, he was ready to play baseball again.

When McGwire had been in his slump, he had taken advice from everyone. He had tried a thousand different strategies at the plate, creating some bad habits and losing his usual swing. In order to succeed, he had to teach himself to hit again.

That spring he worked hard with the A's new hitting coach, Doug Rader. Rader had McGwire crouch down a little farther and get a little closer to the plate. A fan had noticed that over time McGwire had changed the position of his feet and recommended that he return to his old closed, pigeon-toed stance.

Combined with McGwire's new attitude, those subtle changes allowed him to feel comfortable at the plate again. He stayed back on the ball until the last instant, then exploded, his compact swing moving through the hitting zone with incredible speed. The ball began to jump off his bat just as it had during his rookie season.

That was bad news for American League pitchers, who had begun to consider McGwire an easy out. When the 1992 season started and McGwire stepped to the plate, the opposition saw a brand-new player. He even looked different. Over the winter he had grown a goatee.

McGwire got off to a great start, hitting home runs at a pace he hadn't approached since his rookie year. In April alone, he slugged 10 home runs. In May, he followed with 8 more.

Once again, he was on a pace to challenge Roger Maris's home-run record. This time, talk about the record from his fans and the press didn't distract him. Instead, it helped bolster his confidence. He believed in himself again.

Although McGwire's hitting eventually tailed off and he missed several weeks of the season in August and September due to injury, he still finished with 42 home runs and more than 100 RBIs. His batting average soared nearly seventy points, to .268, his second-best mark ever in the major leagues.

Even better, the A's rebounded from their fourth-place finish in 1991 to win another Western Division title. But in a hard-fought series with the Toronto Blue Jays, the A's lost in six games. Like most other A's hitters, McGwire slumped in the series, hitting only .150 with just a single home run. He was disappointed but still viewed the 1992 season positively. He had proved to himself that he was still a potent hitter. During the season, he had hit a home run every 11.1 at bats, one of the best rates in the history of the game.

After the season, he finished fourth in balloting for the American League Most Valuable Player (MVP) award, won an award as baseball's comeback player

Sammy Sosa and Mark McGwire, challengers for the home-run record, share a friendly moment on the field before a game. Sosa has 43 so far, and McGwire has 45.

Before Sosa and the Cubs go head-to-head with McGwire and the Cardinals, the home-run kings share a laugh with the press. Sosa, with 58, and McGwire, with 60, are closing in on the record.

Mark McGwire throws his bat aside and watches his 61st home run—the run that tied Roger Maris's single-season record—soar to the back of Busch Stadium.

The single-season home-run record is broken! McGwire shouts and jumps with triumph as home run number 62 leaves the stadium.

Third-base coach Rene Lachemann whoops it up as McGwire runs his 62nd home-run lap.

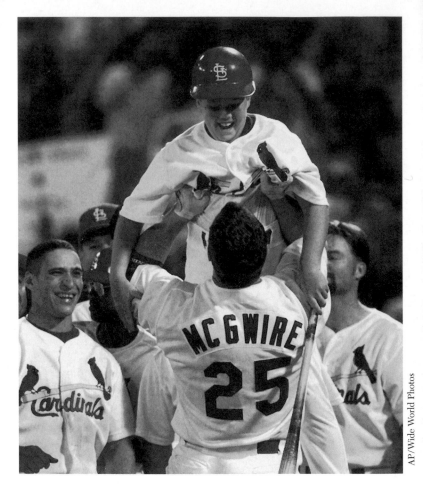

Matthew McGwire enjoys a lift at home plate from his slugger dad after the 62nd home run.

McGwire commemorates the past as he shares his joy with the Maris family after the 62nd homer.

Last but not least... McGwire's final homer of the 1998 season, number 70, gives the world a new record.

Relaxed and enjoying the moment, McGwire jogs the bases for the 70th time.

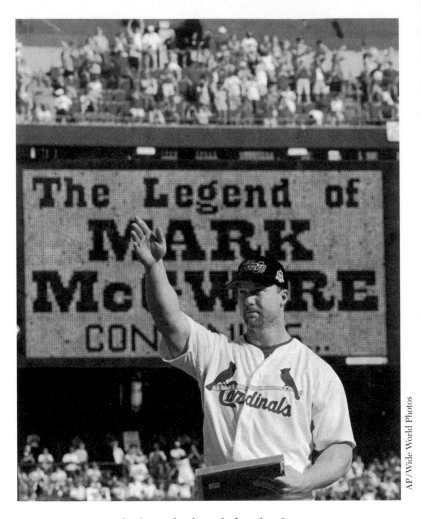

The legend acknowledges his fans.

Mark McGwire's Career Highlights

1987:
Rookie of the Year
Held rookie season record for home runs (49)
Led American League in home runs
Member of All-Star Team

1988:
Member of All-Star Team

1989:
Led league with best home-run ratio (one every 14.8 at bats)

1990:
First player to hit more than 30 home runs during his first four
  seasons
Member of All-Star Team

1992:
Led league with best home-run ratio (one every 11.1 at bats)

1995:
Topped Babe Ruth's home-run ratio (one every 8.5 at bats)
  with 8.1
One of seven players in major league history to hit 30 home
  runs in fewer than 400 at bats

1997:
Hit 58 homers, 3 away from tying the single-season record
Became second player in major league history to hit 50 home
  runs in two consecutive seasons (Babe Ruth was the first)

1998:
Tied, then broke, the 37-year-old record for most home runs
  hit in one season (61), held by Roger Maris, by pounding out
  70 total

Mark McGwire's Year-to-Year Major League Statistics

Year	Club	Games	At Bats	Runs	Hits	2B	3B	HRs	RBIs	Avg.
1986	Oakland	18	53	10	10	1	0	3	9	.189
1987	Oakland	151	557	97	161	28	4	49	118	.289
1988	Oakland	155	550	87	143	22	1	32	99	.260
1989	Oakland	143	490	74	113	17	0	33	95	.231
1990	Oakland	156	523	87	123	16	0	39	108	.235
1991	Oakland	154	483	62	97	22	0	22	75	.201
1992	Oakland	139	467	87	125	22	0	42	104	.268
1993	Oakland	27	84	16	28	6	0	9	24	.333
1994	Oakland	47	135	26	34	3	0	9	25	.252
1995	Oakland	104	317	75	87	13	0	39	90	.274
1996	Oakland	130	423	104	132	21	0	52	113	.312
1997	Oakland	105	366	48	104	24	0	34	81	.284
1997	St. Louis	51	174	38	44	3	0	24	42	.253
1998	St. Louis	155	509	130	152	21	0	70	147	.299
Major League totals		1535	5131	941	1353	219	5	457	1130	.264

of the year, and was named as first baseman on the *Sporting News* major league All-Star team.

McGwire could hardly wait for the 1993 season to begin. His contract with the A's was up, leaving him a free agent, but when Oakland expressed desire for him to stay on, he quickly re-signed. He felt comfortable in Oakland.

During the first few weeks of the 1993 season he proved that his comeback hadn't been a fluke. Despite being hampered by a sore back for a few games, in early May he was leading the team with 9 home runs, 24 RBIs, and a batting average of .333.

But in a game against New York, McGwire began having pain in his left heel. He tried to play on the injury but it only got worse.

Team doctors diagnosed the injury as a bruised heel and strained arch. McGwire tried to treat the injury with rest, but when the pain failed to subside, the A's put McGwire on the disabled list and placed his foot in a cast. Doctors thought that if he stayed off the heel for a while, it would heal on its own.

But when they removed the cast, McGwire was still unable to run without suffering excruciating pain. They tried a cast a second time, but the injury still refused to heal.

McGwire's season was over. For the remainder of the year, he sat watching as his teammates tried to win without him. They couldn't. The A's finished in last place in the Western Division. In late September, with the season nearly over, McGwire underwent surgery on his foot.

McGwire spent the 1993 off-season recovering. His foot began to feel better. He was eager to prove that he was still one of the most dangerous hitters in baseball.

But the long layoff took its toll. McGwire got off to a slow start.

Then his foot began bothering him again. He tried to play through the pain, but the injury affected how he swung the bat. It bothered him to put pressure on the foot as he strode forward during his swing.

For the first half of the year he was in and out of the lineup, playing when he was able. Finally, on July 26, 1994, while running the bases in a game against the California Angels, he suffered another injury to the same foot. The fascia, a sheet of connective tissue that supports the arch, had torn.

McGwire was put on the disabled list once again. He resisted more surgery, afraid that although it might repair the tear it might also leave the foot weaker than before.

In the meantime, the baseball season ground to a halt. On August 11, 1994, the players, who had been playing without a contract with major league baseball, went out on strike. Both sides dug in, and in mid-September, the remainder of the 1994 season was canceled.

For Mark McGwire, it was already over. In late August he had decided to have surgery a second time.

In October he began a long, slow rehabilitation. Working with his brother and A's conditioning coach Bob Alejo, McGwire was determined to do all he could to help the healing process. If the heel went out on him again, he wanted to know that he had done everything possible to prevent the re-injury.

For the first time, McGwire added aerobic exercise, such as jogging, to his program. He had to train his foot to withstand the stress of running. Lifting weights simply hadn't done that.

He began by walking on flat ground for three minutes at a time. Each day, he walked a little farther. He eventually began walking uphill, and finally he began to jog. By the spring, he was running thirty minutes a day and had cut his body fat by half. He felt great.

Now all he needed was the strike to end. Players and owners didn't settle their differences until late April of 1995, and the season didn't get under way until mid-May.

McGwire quickly made up for lost time. He started hitting home runs faster than any player in history.

The past two seasons he had spent on the bench watching had taught him a few things. As he said later, the experience made him "a better mental player." He studied pitchers and began to understand their strategy. Watching his teammates try to hit taught him the importance of being patient at the plate, of waiting to get a good pitch.

When the season started, McGwire was a different hitter. In each at bat, he was "locked in," totally focused on hitting the ball. He rarely chased a ball out of the strike zone, and when he got a good pitch to hit, he rarely missed it. And he wasn't just making contact either. He was crushing the ball. Most of McGwire's home runs were bombs traveling well over 400 feet.

Even though he suffered through a nagging series of minor injuries that caused him to miss more than 30 games, McGwire made the most of each at bat. Despite playing in only 104 games and coming to bat only 317 times, he hit a remarkable 39 home runs, one home run for every eight at bats. No one else in the history of the game had ever done that.

Mark McGwire was back!

Chapter Seven:
1996–1997

Slugger in St. Louis

Despite McGwire's dramatic return to form, the A's failed to challenge for the Western Division title in 1995. Major league baseball had changed its divisional structure, adding a third division in each league and allowing two teams to qualify for "wild card" playoff berths. The A's hadn't come close to being a wild card team either. In the off-season, the team was sold and the new owners fired manager Tony LaRussa and replaced him with Art Howe. It was rebuilding time once again.

For a while it appeared as if the A's might trade McGwire. He was a valuable commodity and the team wanted a number of prospects in return. But baseball was still recovering from the 1994 strike and no team was prepared to offer Oakland fair value in exchange for McGwire.

McGwire continued his hard work during the 1995 off-season and reported to spring training in great shape. He was optimistic about the future of the team and hoped they could turn things around. He wanted to be a part of that.

But only two weeks into 1996 spring training, disaster struck. As he was running the bases he heard a loud pop and immediately felt pain in his right foot. Incredibly, he had suffered the same injury to his right foot that had once plagued his left.

McGwire was crushed. It had taken two operations and two years of hard work for his left foot to heal. McGwire later told a reporter, "I thought about retirement because I didn't want to go through rehab again." But after talking with his friends and family, he reconsidered and decided to keep playing.

This time, his injured foot responded to treatment without surgery. Although McGwire began the season on the disabled list, he returned to the lineup in late April.

He hit as if he had never been out. Day after day, home runs flew off his bat. He was hitting home runs like other players hit singles.

Late in the season, McGwire was approaching a total of 50 home runs. Although Maris's home-run record was out of reach because of the time McGwire missed at the beginning of the season, the press and McGwire's fans began asking him about the record again. He cautioned reporters that "I don't sit here thinking about it because I realize how difficult it is. Hitting a home run is probably the most difficult thing in sports."

Near the end of the 1996 season McGwire belted his 50th home run and finished the year with a remarkable 52.

In the process, he fashioned one of the greatest seasons for any slugger in the history of baseball. He had reached 50 home runs in fewer at bats — 390 — than any hitter in history, including Babe Ruth. For the second year in a row he had hit a home run approximately every 8 at bats. McGwire was even more pleased to finish the year with a .312 batting average, the highest full-season mark of his career. The player whom no one had wanted in 1991 was now at the top of his game.

In 1997, McGwire was in the final year of his contract with the A's. Their rebuilding program was taking time. Although McGwire liked playing in Oakland, he knew the team might not be willing to pay him what he was worth. He also wasn't sure if he wanted to continue playing for a team that had little chance of going to the World Series.

Yet even as the A's struggled, he continued his stellar performance at the plate. At the All-Star break he had already hit 31 home runs. Everyone but McGwire was starting to talk about Roger Maris once again.

It was now an open secret that the A's were looking to trade McGwire for some prospects before his contract expired. But as a ten-year veteran with five years of service with one team, McGwire had the right to approve a trade. He gave permission to the A's to start shopping him around.

Most midseason trades for players are made by teams looking to bolster their lineup for the pennant race. According to baseball's rules, a player must be on the roster of a team by July 31 in order to be eligible for postseason play.

The Toronto Blue Jays and the St. Louis Cardinals both expressed interest in McGwire. McGwire told the A's he would accept a trade to the Cardinals.

As the trade rumors swirled around him, McGwire went into a slump. He hit only three home runs during the month of July.

That had little effect on the desire of the Cardinals to acquire him. Finally, on July 31, 1997, the A's traded McGwire to St. Louis for three prospects.

McGwire was pleased with the deal. He was reunited with Tony LaRussa, who had moved on to become manager of the Cardinals. Furthermore, the club was only seven and a half games out of first place. He was in a pennant race.

But at the same time, the trade meant an adjustment for McGwire. He was separated from his son by more than fifteen hundred miles, he had to find a new place to live, and he had to get to know his new teammates. In addition, McGwire had to adjust to National League pitching. "I'm facing pitchers I've never faced before and playing in surroundings I'm not familiar with," he said.

As a result, McGwire got off to a terrible start. In his first 34 at bats for St. Louis, he had only three hits and one home run.

Yet despite his slump, Cardinals fans didn't boo him. Instead, they cheered loudly every time he stepped to the plate.

McGwire was stunned. Fans in Oakland were laid back. Unless the A's were in a pennant race, the fans hadn't been very enthusiastic, and when McGwire slumped, they jeered him.

The St. Louis fans were different. They were hard-core baseball fans and were thrilled to have McGwire on the team. Never in their history had the Cardinals had a slugger with McGwire's reputation, and the fans understood that he had a lot to get used to.

Sure enough, their patience paid off. After his slow start, McGwire began hitting home runs at a record pace.

Veteran observers were stunned. They had expected McGwire's home-run hitting to tail off in St. Louis. In general, National League ballparks are much bigger than those in the American League and more difficult to hit home runs in.

But nobody hit home runs like Mark McGwire. He hit them so far it didn't matter how big a ballpark was. A 450-foot fly ball was a home run anywhere.

During the last two months of the season, Big Mac, as he was sometimes called, crushed 24 home runs. He closed the season with a rush to finish with a total of 58, the most since Maris set the record at 61 in 1961.

Although the Cardinals failed to make the play-offs, McGwire was surprised to discover that he loved playing in St. Louis. The fans made him feel at home, he liked his teammates, and he enjoyed living in the city.

After hitting so many home runs for the season, many people expected McGwire to cash in and become a free agent. He could easily command the biggest contract in baseball.

But McGwire didn't think that way. Matthew came to visit and he liked St. Louis, too. When McGwire asked his son what he should do, the young boy told him he should stay in St. Louis.

In late September, McGwire and the Cardinals began to work on a deal. After only a few days, they agreed on a three-year contract worth $30 million.

It was a lot of money, but on the open market McGwire probably could have gotten $8 million or $10 million more.

At the press conference to announce the deal, McGwire also divulged his plans to make a $1-million donation to a foundation he had created called the Mark McGwire Foundation for Children. The charitable organization would be dedicated to preventing the sexual abuse of children. When McGwire told the press about his plans, he broke into tears.

Some wondered if McGwire had been sexually abused himself. He assured them that he hadn't. He had decided to start the foundation after a friend, who worked with young victims of sexual abuse, told him stories about the problem. McGwire was moved by what she told him and wanted to help. It was that simple.

Fans in St. Louis and elsewhere were moved by his announcement. Donations to his foundation poured in. McGwire couldn't believe the response.

Only a few years before, the notion that he would show his feelings and break down in tears at a press conference would have been unthinkable. But now, after years of therapy, McGwire was comfortable letting people know how he felt. He liked being Mark McGwire and was humbled by the fact that other people seemed to like him, too, regardless of how many home runs he hit.

McGwire felt a peace in St. Louis that he had never known before. He felt that he had matured, both as a person and as a player.

He couldn't wait for the 1998 season to begin. He wanted to do something special.

Chapter Eight:
1998

Chasing Maris

After blasting 58 home runs in 1997, McGwire privately thought that Maris's record was within his reach. Yet at the same time he knew it would be extremely difficult. He would have to jump out to a quick start, stay healthy, and avoid a major slump. Everything would have to be just about perfect.

Before the season started he asked his son, "Matt, how many home runs do you want me to hit this season?" The boy looked at his father and smiled. "Sixty-five," he said.

McGwire started to laugh. Sixty-two home runs were a lot! But 65, well, that number was almost beyond belief. Still, he told Matt he'd try.

Many observers believed there was a good chance that either McGwire or another big slugger, such as Ken Griffey Jr., would challenge Maris's record in

1998. Many of baseball's best home-run hitters, including McGwire, were just reaching their prime, and the 1998 season was an expansion year. New teams in Arizona and Tampa Bay meant more players in the major leagues. Talent, particularly pitching talent, was diluted. Offense usually went up in expansion years. Maris had set his record in just such a season.

From the moment McGwire arrived at spring training, he was peppered with questions about breaking the record. Repeatedly he told the press that it really wasn't even worth talking about yet. "To have a chance," he said, "I think you have to have fifty home runs by September. If that happens, talk to me then." He wanted to avoid putting any undue strain on himself and hoped to avoid a year-long media circus.

Many people thought that pressure would be the greatest obstacle to breaking the record. When Maris was in pursuit of the record in 1961, he almost buckled under the stress. Some fans resented him for breaking the record once held by the beloved Ruth. Maris received hate mail and was sometimes booed. It got so bad that he hardly slept and his hair fell out. He didn't enjoy his record chase.

Maris had played during an era when there was comparatively little press coverage. After each game, he usually faced only a couple of newspaper reporters and a television crew. That was nothing compared with what was certain to face a challenger to his record. Media coverage has expanded exponentially.

The last time a player had pursued a major record was in 1997, when Cal Ripken Jr. was closing in on Lou Gehrig's record for most consecutive games played. Ripken faced a media onslaught all season long.

The home-run record was different. It was baseball's most cherished and most well known record. Whoever chased Maris was certain to be confronted by even more press coverage than Ripken had experienced.

McGwire began his record chase in the first game of the season. In the fifth inning of a scoreless game against the Los Angeles Dodgers, McGwire came up to bat. The bases were loaded.

Busch Stadium was packed to capacity. As McGwire

stepped up to the plate, everyone in the ballpark stood and cheered.

Dodgers pitcher Ramon Martinez worked carefully. But with the bases loaded and the score tied, he couldn't afford to walk McGwire.

He made a mistake and put a pitch over the middle of the plate. McGwire uncoiled as the pitch approached.

Pow! His bat swept across the plate in a blur and struck the ball solidly. The ball jumped off his bat and soared high into the air, finally coming down well back in the left-field stands, 360 feet from home plate. Home run!

A new record was only 61 home runs away.

McGwire continued his hot hitting in the second game of the season, cracking a game-winning home run in the twelfth inning. Then he homered again in game number three. The next game, he blasted an amazing 430-foot home run against San Diego. The season was less than a week old, and McGwire already had four home runs! All everyone could talk about was Mark McGwire and the home-run record.

Then McGwire's bat went silent. Over the next

nine days he failed to hit a home run. Perhaps, wondered McGwire's fans, talk of breaking Maris's record was premature.

But then McGwire demonstrated that he was never more dangerous than when people began counting him out. On April 14 against the expansion Arizona Diamondbacks, he exploded.

He homered three times. Two of his blasts traveled more than 400 feet.

By the end of the month McGwire had cracked 11 home runs, had knocked in 36 RBIs, and was hitting over .300. National League pitchers were becoming afraid to pitch to him. In only a month they had walked him nearly thirty times. They knew that if they threw McGwire a strike, he might hit a home run. Pitching carefully, and even walking McGwire if they had to, was a much safer strategy.

That approach challenged McGwire. To break the record, he had to remain patient, even when pitchers weren't giving him good pitches to hit. He knew that if he started swinging at bad pitches, he simply couldn't hit many home runs. He had to stay focused.

If he had been younger, it's doubtful whether

McGwire could have retained his concentration. But he had matured and learned a great deal about himself. He now had enough self-confidence to take what the pitchers were giving him. If they made a mistake, he was ready.

He continued to swing a hot bat in May. But McGwire was doing more than just hitting home runs. He was hitting home runs longer, and more often, than anyone else who had ever played the game.

On May 16 in St. Louis, the Cardinals played host to the Florida Marlins, defending world champions. Although the Marlins had since traded away their best players, they still had Livan Hernandez, the 1997 World Series MVP and one of the best young pitchers in baseball.

Hernandez was a challenge to McGwire. Not only was he good, but also McGwire was unfamiliar with him. Most hitters will admit that it is much harder to hit against a pitcher they've never faced before.

But McGwire was locked in. At this point, it didn't matter to him who the pitcher was. He just tried to see the ball and hit it.

Hernandez threw him a pitch up and over the

plate, a hanging slider. McGwire unleashed a mighty swing. The ball hit the fat part of his bat and made a resounding *crack*. Then it took off toward center field, incredibly high and fast.

McGwire stood at the plate for a moment, tossed his bat away, and began his slow trot around the bases. He knew it was a home run. But he could hardly believe how quickly the ball was disappearing from sight. This wasn't just another home run.

Fans all over the ballpark followed the flight of the ball. When it cleared the center fielder's head it was still rising. When it passed the center-field fence, 410 feet from home plate, the ball was still well over 100 feet above the ground.

It finally began its descent, sailing above the screen in center field. Then it banged off a sign on the facade of the second deck, just below the row of luxury boxes that circled the field.

The ball ricocheted into the seats below. The fans cheered and shouted, pointing to where the ball had struck the sign and left a small dent. No one had ever hit a ball that far in Busch Stadium before.

It was later calculated that the ball had struck the sign an incredible 550 feet from home plate! The home run was shown again and again on TV high-light clips all over the country. If anyone had been unaware of Mark McGwire, no one was anymore. A few days later, the Cardinals marked the spot on the sign by sticking a huge Band-Aid over it.

Then McGwire really got hot. When the Cardinals played the Phillies in Philadelphia on May 19, he cracked three home runs once more, becoming the twelfth player in big league history to hit three home runs in one game twice during the same season.

He finished the week with 5 more home runs in only four games. Before the month ended, he slammed 2 more. With the season only one third over, McGwire was nearly halfway to a new record, with 27 home runs! If he kept up the pace, he would end the season with over 80 home runs. He was well ahead of Maris's pace. In fact, he was hitting home runs faster than any man in the history of the game. He wouldn't just break the record. He would shatter it.

Yet despite McGwire's remarkable performance, the Cardinals, whom many observers had picked to win the National League's Central Division, were struggling. Their pitching staff was decimated by injuries, and the other Cardinal hitters weren't performing quite as well as expected. Although McGwire was a one-man wrecking crew, the Cardinals couldn't keep the other teams from scoring. They struggled to play .500 baseball.

Many people wondered if the Cardinals' sub-par performance would adversely affect McGwire's quest. Opposition pitchers could pitch around McGwire without worrying too much about losing. On several occasions in close games, McGwire was walked intentionally without anyone on base. The record was far from a sure thing.

McGwire wasn't alone in the home-run chase, either. Ken Griffey Jr. was also taking aim at Maris's mark, and several other hitters, such as San Diego outfielder Greg Vaughn, were also off to good starts.

But McGwire captured the attention of the nation. Since the baseball strike in 1994, interest in baseball had ebbed. Many longtime fans had turned away from the game, thinking the players were greedy. In the meantime, younger sports fans had become more interested in other sports. Baseball, which had long been considered the national pastime, was in danger of being replaced by pro football or basketball.

Now that was changing. Sparked by interest in McGwire, fans were coming back to the game in droves. Nearly every Cardinals game, both at home and on the road, was a sellout. Fans began showing up at the ballpark early so they could watch McGwire take batting practice. ESPN often cut away from other baseball broadcasts whenever McGwire came to bat.

As many people had predicted, the press converged on McGwire, following his every move. When he took batting practice, they surrounded the batting cage. Before and after every game, McGwire was bombarded with questions. He tried to remain patient, but he grew tired of answering the same questions over and over.

In June, McGwire continued to hit home runs, but at a more human pace. He was still on track to break the record.

But all of a sudden, there was a new challenger to worry about. Chicago Cubs outfielder Sammy Sosa surged into the home-run chase.

At the end of May, Sosa had only 13 home runs,

less than half of McGwire's total. No one expected him to challenge for the record. He was a fine player, but he had never hit more than 40 home runs in a single season. But starting on June 1, he began to smack home runs at a tremendous pace.

During the first eight days of June, Sosa cracked 7 home runs. Then, after failing to hit a home run for four days, he resumed his surge. From June 13 through June 25, he hit a remarkable 12 home runs. His season total stood at 32 home runs, only 3 behind McGwire's 35.

Sosa's sudden torrent of home runs proved to be a blessing in disguise for McGwire. Although most people expected Sosa's home runs to tail off, he still drew some of the attention of the press from McGwire. He also provided the Cardinals' slugger with some extra motivation. With the Cardinals playing poorly, it was hard for Mark to stay focused. But with Sosa moving up from behind, McGwire had one more reason not to let up.

When McGwire cracked a 470-foot home run off Kansas City in an interleague game on the last day of June, he still led the majors with 37. But Sosa homered on the final day of the month, too. It was his

21st for the month, a new record, giving him a total of 33. Ken Griffey Jr. was also keeping pace. He, too, had 33 home runs.

Fans looked forward to seeing all three players in the annual All-Star game, scheduled to be held at Coors Field in Denver. Coors Field, nearly a mile above sea level, has a reputation for being an excellent place to hit home runs because the ball travels farther in the thinner air. The annual home-run derby held the day before drew nearly as much attention as the game itself. Fans anticipated watching the sluggers go head-to-head to hit home runs off batting-practice pitching.

Unfortunately, Sosa withdrew from the competition and game due to a small injury. But with a nationwide television audience tuning in, McGwire smacked the longest home run of the day, a towering 510-foot shot. At the end of the day, though, it was Ken Griffey Jr. who won the competition.

The season was barely half over. Although McGwire was off to a spectacular start, he knew his most challenging days lay just ahead.

Chapter Nine:
July–August 1998

Help from Sammy

After the All-Star game, Mark McGwire began to show signs that the pressure was getting to him. He was impatient at the plate, swinging at balls he couldn't possibly hit as pitchers became even more wary of throwing him a good pitch. At the same time, the press was more demanding than ever. Everywhere McGwire went, someone was sticking a microphone in his face. Going out in public became unpleasant for him.

At press conferences held after nearly every game, McGwire began to get testy. He was uncomfortable with personal questions and was frustrated that the press virtually ignored his teammates or the outcome of the game. When asked a question he had already answered dozens of times, he sometimes rolled his eyes, shook his head, and gave a one-word response.

He complained to the press that he was beginning to feel like a "caged animal." He even decided to stop taking batting practice before every game just to avoid the crush around the batting cage.

He was still hitting home runs, but not nearly as often as he had during the first half of the season. He set the Cardinals' team record with his 44th home run in the 104th game of the season on July 26, but during the next three weeks he hit only 3 more. He was now in an official slump.

At the same time, he suddenly found himself being criticized. A reporter discovered that McGwire was taking a dietary supplement called androstenedione. The substance increases the body's production of the hormone testosterone and is supposed to help increase strength and endurance, particularly when used in combination with weight training.

The use of andro is banned by the NFL and the International Olympic Committee because they feel it gives users an unfair advantage. But baseball has no such policy.

Some writers began to question McGwire's use of

the substance. They believed it tainted his performance on the field and wondered if he would be hitting so many home runs if he weren't taking andro.

The use of dietary supplements by athletes is controversial. During the past few years a variety of supplements have been touted as performance enhancers. Many of these substances have never been tested by the government to prove their safety. For a professional athlete under medical supervision, use of supplements combined with intensive training may well be safe. But even McGwire agrees that young athletes should never use such substances. Taking a pill or a powder is never a substitute for hard work in the gym or on the field.

McGwire was surprised by the controversy. Unlike anabolic steroids, which are muscle-building substances that are known to cause health problems and that are illegal to use without a doctor's prescription, andro is one of many supplements available without prescription. And McGwire didn't believe it helped his play any more than the vitamins and other dietary supplements he was taking. "It's legal," he told the press over and over. "I wouldn't take anything illegal." He explained that he took andro only before working out with weights. He believed it helped pump him up and allowed a more efficient workout. Because his injuries had kept him out of the lineup for so long in the past, he felt that it was important to stay as strong as possible to avoid further injury.

Slowly, the controversy faded. However, McGwire's slump continued. Then he received help from an unlikely source.

In August the Cardinals and Cubs played each other several times. For the first time since their home-run chase began, McGwire and Sammy Sosa were able to spend some time together.

In contrast to McGwire, Sosa was having a great time chasing the record. He seemed to enjoy the attention of the press. He joked and smiled and laughed his way through press conferences. It helped that he wasn't under quite as much scrutiny as McGwire and that the Cubs were still in contention for the divisional title.

The two players first met in St. Louis in early August. They had a chance to talk in private for a few moments and McGwire began to realize that he wasn't the only player who faced pressure. He wasn't alone in his chase to set the record. Both players homered in the same game, Sosa cracking his 44th as McGwire hit number 46.

A week later, the Cardinals traveled to Chicago. McGwire and Sosa spent more time together. Both men were delighted to find that they genuinely liked each other. Although each man wanted to set the record, both openly cheered for the other.

McGwire also talked to some of his friends and teammates about the pressure of the chase. He told a reporter later, "They all told me to enjoy this." He decided he would. He even asked a couple of friends, both professional comedians, for some good lines he could use to respond to questions he had grown tired of hearing. Almost immediately, he began to relax.

Sosa and McGwire each became fans of the other. They bantered back and forth like two old friends. Sosa told the press that "we are going to retire together." Both players realized they weren't in competition with each other. They were in competition only with history. As McGwire later told a reporter, "He [Sammy] made me think even more, 'Hey, this game is fun.' This is a game we love to play."

It didn't matter that one man was black, was from the Caribbean, and spoke Spanish, and that the other was white and from California. Baseball brought them together and they became friends. Fans found such genuine affection between the two players refreshing. McGwire and Sosa seemed to provide proof that professional athletes aren't all selfish and concerned only about money.

And then there was the exciting race for Maris's record. When the two clubs faced each other in Chicago on August 19, McGwire and Sosa were tied with 47 home runs each.

In the fifth inning, Sosa connected off Cardinals pitcher Kent Bottenfield. The crowd at Wrigley Field went crazy. For the first time all year, Mark McGwire was behind another player in the home-run chase.

But in the eighth inning, McGwire came up and cracked his 48th home run. The game entered extra innings, and in the tenth McGwire won the game for St. Louis and took the lead back by hitting his 49th home run.

McGwire's home-run drought was over. The next day, the Cardinals were scheduled to play a doubleheader in New York. McGwire set his sights on home run number 50.

Fifty home runs was a benchmark for McGwire. As he had told the press all year long, he had to hit 50 before he could think about hitting 62.

He now felt as relaxed as he had any time since spring training. He was at peace with himself again and brimming with confidence.

In the seventh inning of game one, Mets pitcher Willie Blair made a mistake. McGwire made him pay.

McGwire didn't get all of the pitch, but he is so strong that sometimes, even when he doesn't hit it perfectly, the ball still leaves the park. He drove the ball into left field where it easily cleared the fence, landing in the stands 369 feet from home plate, one of his shortest home runs of the season. He became the first player ever to hit 50 or more home runs in each of three consecutive seasons.

The crowd at Shea Stadium honored him with a standing ovation. McGwire, who usually ran around the bases after a home run as if he were embarrassed, couldn't contain his happiness. He thrust his right arm into the air in celebration, then clapped as he toured the bases. Rounding third, he raised his arm in celebration again. He was having fun, and he didn't mind sharing his feelings with everyone.

He capped the day by leading off the second game with another home run, number 51. After the doubleheader, he expressed pleasure at his accomplishment. "I'm pretty proud of it," he said. Now he felt comfortable talking about the record. "I have a shot," he told reporters, "but it's going to be tough."

After all, McGwire wasn't the only man chasing history.

Chapter Ten:
August–September 1998

Sixty . . .

McGwire and Sosa had captured the collective imagination of the nation. Each man rose to the challenge. Whenever one hit a home run, the other seemed to answer with a home run of his own.

On August 21, the day after McGwire connected for 50 and 51 against the Mets, Sosa slammed number 49. McGwire answered the challenge by hitting number 52 the next day.

Now it was Sosa's turn. He cracked 2 home runs in Houston to draw within one of McGwire. But that same night McGwire blasted home run 53.

Both men then went two days without knocking the ball over the fence before Sosa hit number 52 in Cincinnati. Miles away, McGwire responded a few moments later by hitting number 54, an overwhelming 500-foot blast to center field at Busch Stadium off Florida pitcher Justin Speier.

The entire nation — and a good portion of the baseball-playing world — was mesmerized by the contest between the two players. People felt as if they knew each man. Kids all over the country began to imitate the two stars, skipping down the first base line after hitting a home run, like Sosa, or nonchalantly flicking the bat over their shoulder like McGwire.

McGwire failed to homer for three days. Sosa cracked number 53 on August 28. On Sunday, August 30, Sosa smacked number 54 to tie McGwire again.

The Cardinals-Braves game was the featured broadcast on ESPN that Sunday night. Baseball fans everywhere tuned in to see if McGwire could keep pace.

It was a close, hard-fought game that entered extra innings. When Atlanta scored twice in the top of the eleventh inning, it looked as if McGwire would end the day without a home run. Several St. Louis hitters would have to get on base for McGwire to receive another at bat.

But that's exactly what happened. McGwire strode

to the plate with two teammates on board, nearly fifty thousand Cardinals fans on their feet screaming themselves hoarse, and virtually every baseball fan in America watching on television.

Cagey veteran Dennis Martinez, winner of more than two hundred major league games, was on the mound for the Braves. That didn't matter to Mark McGwire.

He saw the ball and hit it. *Boom!* The ball rocketed off his bat to dead center field and landed 500 feet away. Home run number 55! Game over! Cardinals win, 8–7!

The blast tied the National League home-run record, previously set by Hack Wilson. "I didn't even know that was the record," said McGwire afterward.

But he had precious little time to enjoy the mark. The very next day, Sammy Sosa tied up the race again. Entering September, each man had 55 home runs. Who would come out on top was anyone's guess.

The Cardinals next traveled to Florida. Marlins fans packed the ballpark. Since winning the World

Series, their best players had been traded away and the team was playing poorly. Having Mark McGwire in town was the highlight of the season.

He didn't let them down. In the seventh inning he drove a home run deep into center field. Although the homer put the Marlins down by five runs, Florida fans didn't care. They cheered so long and so loudly that McGwire had to leave the dugout and take a curtain call to get them to stop.

Then, two innings later, he did it again, hitting a home run to almost the exact same spot. Once more, he was called from the dugout to accept the cheers of the crowd.

The two home runs were his ninth and tenth of the past two weeks. No one wondered anymore whether Mark McGwire could handle the pressure of the home-run chase.

The next day he duplicated his effort, cracking 2 more home runs against the Marlins and giving two more curtain calls. In the past fifteen days he had hit an incredible 12 home runs! With 59 home runs for the year and nearly a month left in the season, it was no longer a question of if the record would be broken, but when and by whom. Sosa now had 56 home runs himself.

He added one to that total two days later as McGwire remained stuck on number 59. Each player was pushing the other to perform at the very best of his ability.

Then, on September 5, against Cincinnati, McGwire tied Babe Ruth's best by smacking his 60th home run in the first inning. His teammates greeted him in front of the dugout, pounding fists and exchanging playful punches to the stomach — McGwire's standard method of celebrating.

For the remainder of the game, Cardinals fans pleaded with him to blast number 61, but he didn't. Meanwhile, in Pittsburgh, Sammy Sosa cracked his 58th homer.

The balls McGwire would hit to tie and break Maris's mark were certain to become some of the most valuable pieces of memorabilia in baseball history. Some people had already offered a million dollars for home-run ball number 62. Every fan in the ballpark would be trying to get hold of it.

In anticipation of the record-setting hit, major

league baseball officials and the Cardinals made some special arrangements. In order to identify the baseball in question, they decided that every time McGwire came to the plate, the umpire would put into play some specially marked baseballs. That way, there would be no argument over the authenticity of the record ball.

Major league baseball officials and the Cardinals also planned to hold a special ceremony after the game. They even invited Roger Maris's widow and children to attend as their guests.

Maris was an important figure to McGwire. The Yankee star, who ended his career with the Cardinals, was often overlooked by baseball fans. A quiet, private man, Maris was never as beloved as Babe Ruth.

But McGwire felt a special kinship with Maris. "I can't imagine what he went through in New York City," said McGwire of Maris's pursuit of Ruth's mark in 1961. "I truly believe he's watching me. Hopefully, some day when I pass away I'll get to meet him."

Although Mrs. Maris was hospitalized with a heart problem, the Maris children were in attendance when McGwire took to the field on Sunday, September 6. He met with them before the game and told them their father was in his heart.

His first two times up, McGwire lined out and walked. His third time up was in the sixth inning, and for the third time that day all the fans in the park rose to their feet.

McGwire turned on the first pitch thrown by Cincinnati's Bret Tomko and drove it down the left-field line. McGwire stood at the plate after hitting the ball and twisted his body as he watched it clear the fence — foul. He then struck out. In a later at bat, he grounded out to second. Number 61 would have to wait at least one more day.

That was fine with almost everyone. Because guess who was coming to St. Louis to play a two-game series with the Cardinals? Sammy Sosa and the Chicago Cubs. America could hardly wait.

Chapter Eleven:
September 7, 1998

Sixty-One . . .

Before the first game of the series on September 7, 1998, Mark McGwire and Sammy Sosa sat next to each other at a press conference, the first time they had appeared together anywhere but on the baseball field. They didn't seem to be collapsing under the pressure. They looked like two good friends who enjoyed being in each other's company.

As the press peppered them with questions, they handled the attention in stride and responded with a series of lighthearted answers. Since Sosa was always telling the press that McGwire was "the man," a reporter asked which of them was really "the man."

They were taken aback for a moment before Sosa, smiling, pointed at McGwire and quipped, "He is 'the man' in the United States. I am 'the man' in the

Dominican Republic." Then both men laughed and pounded each other on the back.

But McGwire set the tone of their meeting. Near the end of the press conference, someone asked who the two men thought would end the year with the most home runs. McGwire jumped to answer. "Wouldn't it be great," he said, "if we tied?"

Then, when someone asked him if he was excited, he laughed incredulously and added, "How can you not be excited? Your heart's not beating if you're not excited about today and tomorrow."

After the conference, both players began preparing for the game. McGwire made certain he did everything exactly as he had done all year long. He was superstitious and didn't want to do anything differently.

As soon as he stepped onto the field for batting practice, nearly two hours before the start of the game, the capacity crowd at Busch Stadium was on its feet.

They weren't disappointed. After bunting the first batting-practice pitch, McGwire lined the next three balls into the stands in left field. If he was feeling any pressure, it certainly wasn't showing.

The Cubs came to bat in the top of the first. When Sammy Sosa stepped to the plate, the crowd stood and cheered for him, acknowledging his role in the historic drama they felt privileged to be a part of. He popped up to McGwire at first base to end the inning.

Then the Cardinals came to bat. As the Cardinals' first hitter was retired, McGwire, scheduled to hit third, grabbed his bat. As he did, a familiar figure bounced into the dugout. McGwire's ex-wife and her husband had agreed to let Matthew McGwire be at the ballpark to serve as batboy the day his father tried to make history. The boy had arrived at the park and pulled on his uniform just in time to greet his father before he stepped into the on-deck circle. McGwire gave his son a big bear hug, told him he loved him, and walked onto the field.

He swung the bat nervously in the on-deck circle for a moment, watching his teammate make an out. Then he stepped up to the plate.

Busch Stadium erupted in cheers as he dug in and tried to concentrate. Cubs pitcher Mike Morgan toed the rubber and looked for the signal from catcher Scott Servais. Morgan tried to concentrate, too. The Cubs were still in the fight for the playoffs and every game and every run was important.

Morgan wound up and threw a slider. McGwire saw the pitch coming and cut loose, taking a gigantic cut.

Whiff! His bat rocketed through the strike zone. The small break on the slider was just enough to make him miss.

The crowd roared in disappointment for a moment, and then the cheers began to build once more. Morgan looked in again, paused, and began his windup.

It was a fastball. Morgan meant to throw the ball down and away, but he missed his spot. The pitch was a strike, just above the waist and on the inner half of the plate.

Once more McGwire took a mighty cut at the ball. This time he connected.

On the mound, Mike Morgan spun around and looked up. The ball was nearly launched into orbit. It sailed high and deep toward left field.

McGwire knew it was gone. He paused at home plate for a moment, flicked his bat like a toothpick over his shoulder, and watched as the ball sailed over the fence and clattered off the Plexiglas window of a luxury box deep in left field, 430 feet from home plate. Then he raised his huge arms in triumph and, with a wide grin breaking out on his face, started his tour of the bases for the 61st time that season.

As he rounded first, he shook hands with first-base coach Dave McKay, then Cubs first baseman Mark Grace slapped his hand. In right field, Sammy Sosa applauded into his mitt.

Every fan in the ballpark joined them in celebration. When McGwire crossed the plate he was met by Matt, whom he lifted into the air in another giant hug before setting him back down, the boy chuckling with delight. Then the son dutifully carried his father's bat back toward the dugout.

McGwire pointed to his father in the stands. He had hit his record-tying 61st home run on his father's sixty-first birthday! He also pointed to the Maris family in the stands and blew a soft kiss into the air, letting them know he was thinking about their father.

McGwire's teammates poured out of the dugout,

and he playfully exchanged punches and high fives with them, then waved to the crowd.

The cheering continued for a full five minutes. McGwire acknowledged the applause. He even looked out to Sammy Sosa and imitated Sosa's trademark pounding of the chest.

McGwire was now tied with Roger Maris for the most home runs ever hit in a single season. But he had accomplished his mark in twenty-five fewer games and 142 fewer at bats than the Yankee star. With nearly three weeks remaining in the season, he was only one swing away from history. The entire world was now waiting for number 62.

Chapter Twelve:
September 8, 1998

Sixty-Two . . .

Everyone at Busch Stadium on September 7 was hoping that McGwire would hit number 62 later in the game, but he failed to homer for a second time in the Cardinals' 3–2 victory. Still, the stage was now set for a new record.

Everyone in America wanted to be at the game the following evening, September 8, 1998. Fans began showing up at the park hours before the gates opened. Bleacher seats that cost less than ten dollars were being sold for more than four hundred dollars. Good seats were selling for thousands of dollars. Hundreds of reporters and television camera crews joined the crush of 48,688 fans for the chance to witness history.

St. Louis fans were particularly eager to see McGwire set the record that night. The game was the last of the home stand. Afterward, the Cardinals would go on a long road trip. This game would probably be McGwire's only chance to set the record in front of his home crowd.

In the midst of such excitement, Mark McGwire was the most relaxed man in the ballpark. He was utterly confident. He felt locked in at the plate. Before the game he met with representatives from the Baseball Hall of Fame, who had brought along the bat Maris used to hit his 61st home run. McGwire held the bat in his huge hands for a moment, then touched it to his heart for good luck.

The Fox television network preempted its regular programming to show the game to the entire country. Millions of people stayed home that night to watch Mark McGwire.

He stepped to the plate in the first inning to the now-routine roars of the crowd. Cubs pitcher Steve Trachsel pitched carefully. He wanted to get McGwire out and win the game for his team. He threw three consecutive balls. With the count 3 and 0, his next pitch was on the corner.

Usually, McGwire doesn't swing when the count is 3 and 0, but this time he decided to risk it. He took a mighty cut but was fooled by the pitch. He barely made contact and bounced into an easy ground out. Disappointed fans sat back down. But the night was still young.

He came to bat in the fourth inning for the second time that night. Once more, he was wrapped in the cheers of the crowd. He looked out at pitcher Steve Trachsel and tried to think only of the ball about to be thrown in his direction.

Trachsel wound up quickly and threw. The pitch was a strike at the knees, but over the middle of the plate. McGwire uncoiled and swung, turning on the ball with all his might.

Crack! The ball hit the fat part of the bat and took off on a line toward left field.

There was no doubt that McGwire had hit the ball hard enough to leave the ballpark. The only question was whether or not it would be high enough to clear the fence.

He paused for a moment at the end of his swing and followed the flight of the ball. Then, realizing the ball might not clear the fence, he began to sprint.

He needn't have worried. He had taken only a few steps down the line when the ball shot over the fence, hit the facade in front of the first deck, and fell behind the outfield wall.

Home run number 62! Mark McGwire had broken the record! As it happened, at 341 feet, the most important home run of the season was also McGwire's shortest.

As soon as he saw the ball leave the field, McGwire raised his arms in the air and slowed to a trot. First-base coach Dave McKay greeted him at first.

In his excitement, McGwire skipped over the base, missing it completely. McKay reached out and grabbed him. McGwire, in a joyous daze, turned back, stepped on first, and resumed his triumphant tour of the bases.

As he did, every Cub infielder clapped him on the back, slapped his hand, or embraced him as he ran for home. It didn't matter that he played for a different team. They respected his accomplishment. In right field, Sammy Sosa dropped his glove and applauded loudly. The stands were in an uproar, and the cheers of the crowd could be heard throughout downtown St. Louis.

As McGwire approached home, he touched his chest and pointed to the sky in acknowledgment of

Roger Maris. Then Cubs catcher Scott Servais came forward to congratulate him. McGwire hugged him, then ended his long journey and stamped on home plate.

His son was there to greet him, still holding the bat with which his father had made history. McGwire lifted the boy high into the air and shook him while Matt McGwire grinned widely. Then he lowered the boy to the ground and was enveloped by his teammates, some of whom raced across the field from the bull pen to join in the celebration. McGwire hugged everybody and anybody he could reach. He felt nothing but pure joy, and he wanted to share that feeling with everyone.

Sammy Sosa ran in from right field to show his respect for the new home-run king. When McGwire met Sosa he lifted him into the air just as he had his young son, and the two players beamed at each other. Then he set Sosa down and the two high-fived and playfully punched each other in the stomach. McGwire showed his respect for Sosa by imitating the Cubs slugger's trademark celebration gesture, pounding his chest and blowing a kiss with two fingers. The two men then embraced once more, and

Sosa yelled into McGwire's ear, "Now you can go home, relax, and wait for me. Don't get too far ahead, I'll be there soon." McGwire just smiled.

The celebration continued. McGwire sprinted over to the stands adjacent to the Cardinals' dugout, climbed over the barrier, and found the Maris family. He hugged the children of the former home-run king and told them once again that their father was in his heart. Then he dashed back onto the field, waved his arms, and blew kisses to the crowd. They cheered and roared some more.

Someone handed him a microphone, and McGwire briefly addressed the crowd. "To my family, my son, the Cubs, Sammy Sosa. It's unbelievable. Thank you, St. Louis!"

The applause continued for a full eleven minutes before the game resumed. For McGwire, the remainder of the evening passed in a blur. His next two times up, he walked. The Cardinals won, 6–3.

After the game, the Cardinals held another celebration on the field. Baseball commissioner Bud Selig awarded McGwire the first Commissioner's Historical Achievement Award, his teammates gave him a plaque, and the Cardinals gave him a 1962

"Cardinal Red" Corvette sports car in honor of home run number 62.

A member of the Cardinals grounds crew, Tim Forneris, had retrieved the ball from behind the fence. He presented it to McGwire, saying, "Mr. McGwire, I believe I have something that belongs to you." McGwire then spoke briefly to the crowd, thanking everyone and repeating "Thank you, St. Louis," before climbing into the back of the car and being driven around the field, where he waved to the crowd, still thanking them over and over again.

At the press conference, McGwire got a chance to catch his breath. But he still couldn't believe what had just happened.

"I'm almost speechless," he said. "I hit a ball that just disappeared on me. The whole country has been involved in this. Thanks to Babe, Roger, and everybody who's watching up there. It's such an incredible feeling. I can't believe I did it."

Millions of baseball fans shared his incredulity. McGwire had done what many had thought was impossible.

Chapter Thirteen:
September 8–September 27, 1998

Seventy!

When the press conference ended, McGwire joined his teammates on a flight to Cincinnati, where the Cardinals were scheduled to play the next night. He had wanted to take the night off, but when he realized that the game was sold out because of him, he decided to play. He knew that he had an obligation to the fans.

Everyone wondered whether he could hold on and win the race with Sosa. With three weeks left in the season, there was plenty of time for both men to hit a lot more home runs.

McGwire failed to homer during the next few days as his accomplishment sunk in. In the meantime, Sammy Sosa demonstrated that although McGwire may have been the first man to hit 62 home runs, he was still going to try to set a record himself.

Sosa cracked four home runs in three days to draw into a tie with McGwire. Suddenly, it seemed as if McGwire decided it was time to hit home runs again.

Once more, the two men engaged in a historic battle, matching each other home run for home run. Two days after Sosa cracked number 62, McGwire hit number 63. Sosa tied him one day later, then McGwire surged ahead in the race again by smacking numbers 64 and 65.

Baseball fans were enthralled. It was amazing enough for one man to break the record, but for two to do it, and then to battle each other game by game for the last few weeks of the season, was incredible.

With only three games left in the season, both players had 65 home runs. Perhaps McGwire's wish for a tie was going to hold up.

But on the evening of Friday, September 25, Sosa blasted a monstrous 462-foot blast in the Astrodome off Houston pitcher Jose Lima to take the lead in the home-run race for the second time all season.

Yet once more, he held his lead for less than an hour. Forty-six minutes later, in St. Louis, McGwire came up to bat against Montreal pitcher Shayne Bennett.

He turned on a ball and hit it long and high down the left-field line. He stood at the plate, twisting his body and trying to will the ball fair, but it landed just a foot or two foul. It looked as if Sosa would hold the lead.

Then, incredibly, McGwire hit the next pitch to almost the same spot. This time, the ball was fair. The two men were tied again!

The next day, McGwire tested the borders of belief. He hit two more home runs while Sosa was shut out. With one day left in the season, Mark McGwire had hit 68 home runs.

Busch Stadium was packed for the final game of the season. Everyone wanted one more look at Mark McGwire.

In a press conference before the game, McGwire was asked if he would be disappointed if Sosa were to catch him. Mark scoffed at the notion.

"What he and I have done," he said, "nobody

should be disappointed. We're two guys that have done something that's never been done. It's remarkable. Whatever happens, no one should be disappointed. We're just two guys that really enjoy this game of baseball." Then McGwire went out and showed how much he really did enjoy the game.

After singling in his first at bat, he came up for the second time, in the third inning.

Boom! The ball sailed deep to left field and came to rest just below a huge sign for McDonald's that read Big Mac Land. Home run 69.

His next time up, he walked. Then, in the seventh, he came to bat against rookie pitcher Carl Pavano.

More than forty-eight thousand fans screamed and yelled and prayed for another home run. And in this most remarkable of seasons, McGwire answered those prayers.

He ripped a vicious line drive down the left-field line, almost identical to his blast for home run number 62. The ball raced out of the park and crashed into a private box just above the fence.

Home run 70!

The ovation that followed eclipsed the other 69

McGwire had already received that season. In the football stadium next to the ballpark, the St. Louis Rams were playing football. The roar was so loud that the players couldn't hear the quarterback and the team had to take a delay-of-game penalty!

For the last time of the season, Mark McGwire rounded the bases riding the applause of his fans.

After the game, a 6–5 St. Louis win, McGwire took to the field to thank his fans again.

"This is a season I'll never forget," he said, "and I hope no one in baseball will ever forget. Thank you."

Then, the season done, he held his final press conference.

"What Sammy and I have done for the last two months has been magical," he said. "If we've brought people back to baseball, so be it. I'm just a normal person who has a talent to play the game."

He reminded the press that only a few years before he had almost been ready to quit playing baseball. "I don't think you can use your mind any more playing this game of baseball than I have," he said. "It proved to me that I can overcome almost anything I want to overcome with the strength of my mind. Seventy home runs is unheard-of. I'm in awe of myself right now."

McGwire had learned a lot since those days he had considered retirement.

"If you put your mind to something," he said simply, "it can happen."

Mark McGwire proved it seventy different times. He set a record, and became a person, to be proud of.